Standly finds his tribe

Standly finds his tribe

A redwood's story

Kelly Taaffe

In loving memory of my darling Pepper,
whose spirit lives on in the great redwoods

"The clearest way into the Universe is through a forest wilderness."

—John Muir

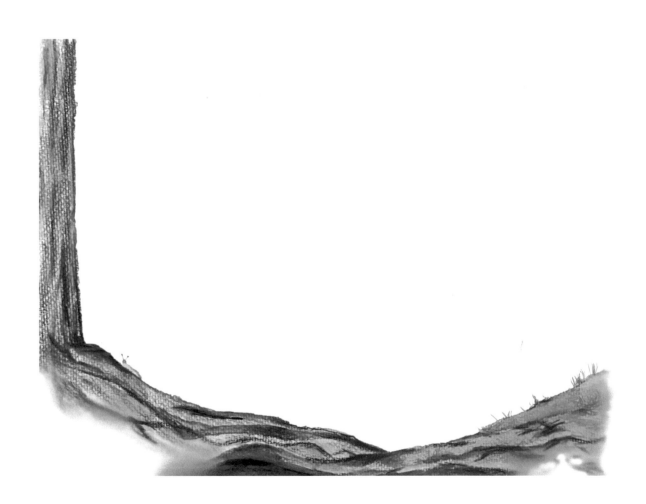

There once was a great tree family
held together by their roots in a valley.

Two parents, some aunts,
some uncles, and kids,
and grandparents who held the soil firmly.

For ages they stood —
as do the redwoods,
calmly collecting the light that they could.

And as the sun rose high one day,
a little stem sprouted beneath a bright ray.

It heightened its reach and took a great stretch,
basking in life and its very first breath.

"Standly, we'll call him,"
said the sprout's mom and dad.
"Standly he'll be,"
echoed each tree in the land.

He grew and he thrived,
through day and through night.

His branches spread vast,
like wings taking flight.

One morning he woke
on a day like the others,
but something had changed:
He saw far fewer colors.

The green forest floor had a dark hint of gray,
for a big tree beside him now stood in his way.

"What nonsense!" he thought,
rustling his leaves.
"I can't do without light!
This is hard to believe."

Standly lowered his gaze to the shadowy ground,
feeling slightly uneasy — and kind of unwound.

Yet just as his branches
began to feel weak,
a voice from behind him
started to speak:

"Standly," said his mother,
as she stood tall and proud,
"It's high time you learned
why we live in this crowd."

"You see, my sweet sapling,
redwoods always thrive.
And the reason for that
is because of our tribe."

"After all, Standly Sequoia Sempervirens
(for that is your name in full),
your roots link to mine,
and mine link to them all.

So never you worry
about shadows or rain,
because family helps you,
and family remains."

Standly breathed in
a big gust of air,
and grew filled with peace
with the trees everywhere.

And when the time came,
that new saplings emerged,
Standly taught each one of them
all that he had learned.

About redwood trees

Coastal redwoods grow taller than any other tree in the world. And while their roots aren't very deep, they stay strong by gathering together in families. They are incredibly hardy, with built-in protection against bugs — and even wildfires.

Sequoia sempervirens (that's their scientific name) are among the oldest living things on the planet. You can find them in parts of Northern California and Oregon, where the trees enjoy a comfortable, foggy climate.

CPSIA information can be obtained
at www.ICGtesting.com
Printed in the USA
LVRC090814250222
711906LV00011B/51